Changes
Home Sweet Home

by Liz Gogerly

HODDER
Wayland

an imprint of Hodder Children's Books

Text copyright © 2003 Hodder Wayland

Project manager: Liz Gogerly
Designer: Peta Morey
Picture Research: Shelley Noronha at Glass Onion Pictures
Consultant: Norah Granger

Published in 2003 by Hodder Wayland, an imprint of Hodder Children's Books

British Library Cataloguing in Publication Data
Gogerly, Liz
Home sweet home. - (Changes ; 5)
1. Dwellings - Great Britain - History - 19th century - Juvenile literature
2. Dwellings - Great Britain - History - 20th century - Juvenile literature
3. Great Britain - Social life and customs - 19th century - Juvenile literature
4. Great Britain - Social life and customs - 20th century - Juvenile literature
I.Title 392.3'6'0941'09034

ISBN 0 7502 3969 7

Printed and bound in Hong Kong by Wing King Tong

Hodder Children's Books
A division of Hodder Headline Limited
338 Euston Road, London NW1 3BH

PICTURE ACKNOWLEDGEMENTS:
The publisher would like to thank the following for allowing their pictures to be used in this publication:
AKG 11 (bottom); Bridgeman Art Library /Cheltenham Art Gallery and Museums, UK 8 (top) /Hamburg Kunsthalle, Germany 10 (top); Camera Press 10 (bottom); Corbis 8 (bottom), 19 (top); D.I.Y Photo Library 16 (bottom); Mary Evans 7 (top), 17 (top); Eye Ubiquitous 4 (bottom); Format Partners/ Ulrike Preuss 19 (bottom); Angela Hampton 14 (bottom); Hodder Wayland Picture Library 7 (bottom) /Angus Blackburn 18 (bottom); Hulton Getty cover (inset), 4 (top),13 (bottom); Yiorgos Nikiteas 6 (bottom); Robert Opie (title), 12 (top), 17 (bottom); Popperfoto 6 (top), 9 (bottom); Public Record Office 9 (top), 13 (top); Topham Picturepoint 5 (top and bottom), 15 (right), 18 (top); V & A Picture Library 16 (top); Zul Mukhida cover (main), 12 (bottom)

Contents

Different Kinds of Homes   4

Living Rooms   6

Cooking in the Kitchen   8

Bedrooms Through the Ages   10

Bathrooms and Toilets   12

Home Comforts   14

Decoration and Furniture   16

A Space Outside   18

Notes for Parents and Teachers   20

About the Photos   20

Glossary   22

Further Information   23

Index   24

WATER HEATING BY
ELECTRICITY WITH THE
SADIA
WATER HEATER
Safety is

Different Kinds of Homes

People live in all kinds of homes. People can live in houses, **bungalows**, cottages, flats or caravans. These can be big or small. It does not matter where you live as long as it feels safe and **secure**. Homes in the past were different but they also felt like 'home sweet home'.

In **Victorian** and **Edwardian** times the poorest people usually lived in houses like those in the photograph. They were built very close together in narrow streets. They were often damp and dark inside. Areas of housing like this were often called **slums**.

In the 1930s many new homes were built. These had bigger rooms and more space for all the family. Houses like these usually had small gardens at the front and back.

By the 1960s there was not much space left in towns and cities for new homes. **High-rise** blocks of flats seemed a good way of using space. How do you think people got to their flat?

Living Rooms

The living room, or the lounge, is where most people **relax** and enjoy themselves. You can play games or watch television. You can read a book or do school work. Some people eat their meals in the living room too. In the past the living room was also where people **relaxed**.

This **Victorian** family was probably quite rich as they have a large living room. They did not have television or radios in those days so people entertained themselves. This family is listening to a woman play the piano.

This photograph was probably taken in about 1930. This family lived in one room. They did everything in this room. They cooked, ate and slept here. It must have been difficult to **relax** sometimes.

This family from the 1940s is **relaxing** by the fire. Until television became popular most people sat around the fireplace to read or listen to the radio. Can you see what else this family did in this room?

Cooking in the Kitchen

The kitchen is also known as the 'heart of the home'. In the past it was often the busiest room in the house. As well as cooking and eating, families talked and kept warm beside the stove. Kitchens have changed over the years. Now that we have **electrical appliances** cooking is quicker and easier.

This is how a **Victorian** kitchen would have looked in a larger home. The fire in the **cast-iron range** was kept going all day. People used it to boil water for drinking and washing. They also used it for cooking.

Even in the 1940s many homes did not have a sink in the kitchen. People did their washing-up and cleaned their clothes in the **scullery**. This was a room behind the kitchen.

This family from the 1960s has a **modern** kitchen. The cupboards are **fitted** and there is a sink for doing the washing-up. There is also a fridge. Everything is bright and clean.

Bedrooms Through the Ages

Bedrooms are no longer just places to sleep. Most children keep their toys and games in their bedrooms. So it is a great place to play when friends come round. Some young people also have computers and televisions in their rooms.

Children from more well-off **Victorian** families often slept in the **nursery**. They had lessons and ate their meals there too. They did not see their parents very often. It must have been lonely sometimes.

In the past many families were much bigger. You would have been very lucky to have a bedroom all to yourself. These sisters from the 1940s had to share their bed too.

In the 1950s younger people's bedrooms became more exciting places. Many teenagers had a **record player**. Often the only place they were allowed to play loud music was in their bedroom.

Bathrooms and Toilets

Nowadays most homes have a bath and shower with hot water. In **Victorian** times many poor homes had no water supply at all. People had to carry water from a tap in the street. Later many homes had one tap for cold water in the **scullery** or kitchen. The water had to be heated on a **cast-iron range** or **stove**.

WATER HEATING BY ELECTRICITY WITH THE **SADIA** WATER HEATER *is Safety with Economy*

In the 1920s only a few people had a bathroom with hot water. If they did they had an electric heater. The water was poured straight into the bath from a **tank** above.

By the 1940s many people still did not have a bathroom. They had to wash in a tin tub next to the fire. The whole family often bathed in the same water.

These boys from the 1950s are playing in the outside toilet. Even by this time some people did not have an indoor toilet. At this time many people used old newspapers as toilet paper.

Home Comforts

Home comforts are the things that make life easier and help us to **relax**. In **modern** homes we have **electrical appliances** like dishwashers and **microwaves** that save us time. We have televisions and radios that bring entertainment into our homes. We also have **central heating** that keeps us warm.

Victorian homes did not have **central heating**. Most families had fires or **cast-iron ranges** to keep them warm. People in more well-off homes had oil heaters like the one in this **advertisement**. These did not heat the whole house and some rooms always felt cold.

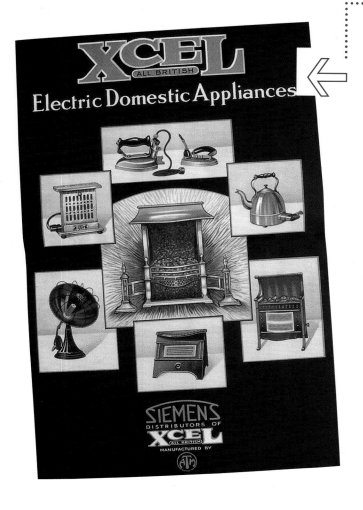

By the 1930s **electrical appliances** were becoming popular. These were expensive so something like an electric fire was a luxury! Can you name any of the things in this **advertisement**?

This woman from the 1950s looks pleased with her new vacuum cleaner. By this time more people could afford **electrical appliances**. Until then many people used brushes to clean their carpets and homes.

Decoration and Furniture

These days people enjoy decorating their homes in different styles. In the shops there are lots of coloured paints and **wallpapers**. There are also many styles of furniture made from different kinds of **material**. In the past people did not have as much choice.

Most **Victorian** homes had lots of dark, heavy furniture made of wood. Curtains were usually made from heavy **material** to help keep out the cold. Walls were usually painted in dark colours or covered with **wallpaper**.

By the 1920s most homes looked lighter and less **cluttered**. Now that some people had electricity their homes were warmer and curtains were made from lighter **material**. Do you prefer the **Victorian** or 1920s style?

In the 1950s people became more interested in painting and decorating their own homes. This magazine is one of the first **do-it-yourself** (DIY) magazines.

Homemaker
THE PRACTICAL HOW-TO-DO-IT *MONTHLY*

Packed with *NEW* ideas for better homemaking
FREE inside!
Homemaker COLOUR SCHEMER

N°I
MARCH 1959
1/3

A Space Outside

In this modern garden there is a lawn and a patio. There are tubs of flowers and trees in the borders. When the weather is warm the family can sit outside on the garden furniture. Through the ages the space outside the home was used in many different ways.

These women from 1922 are in their **back-yards**. This is how the outside space would have looked for the **Victorian** and **Edwardian** homes on page 4. In this small space there was the outside toilet and just enough room to hang out the washing.

During the **Second World War** there was not enough food in the shops to eat. Many people dug up their gardens so they could grow vegetables like potatoes and carrots.

Many flats were built with **balconies** so people had somewhere to get fresh-air. These girls from the 1980s are drying their washing on their **balcony**. Other people put pots of flowers and garden furniture out there.

Notes for Parents and Teachers

Changes and the National Curriculum

The books in this series have been chosen so that children can learn more about the way of life of people in the past. Titles such as *A Bite to Eat, Beside the Sea, Dressing Up, Home Sweet Home, School Days* and *Toys and Games* present children with subjects they already know about from their own experiences of life. As such these books may be enjoyed at home or in school, as they satisfy a number of requirements for the History Programme of Study at Key Stage 1.

These books combine categories from 'Knowledge, skills and understanding' and 'Breadth of study' as required by the National Curriculum. In each spread, the photographs are presented in chronological order. The first photograph is a modern picture that the child should recognize. The following pictures are all historical. Where possible, a wide variety of pictures, including paintings, posters, artefacts and advertisements, have been selected. In this way children can see the different ways in which the past is represented. A lively selection of pictures also helps to develop the children's skills of observation. In turn, this will encourage them to ask questions and discuss their own ideas.

, The text is informative and raises questions for the children to talk about in class or at home. It is supported by further information about the historical photographs (see right). Once the children are familiar with the photographs you could ask them to guess when the pictures were taken – if it isn't mentioned in the text. By looking at clues such as clothes, hairstyles, style of buildings and vehicles they might be able to make reasonable guesses. There are further questions to ask your child or class on the right.

About the Photos

Different Kinds of Home
Pages 4–5

A slum in the East End of London in 1912.
Questions to ask:
- How many street lights can you see in this picture?
- Do you think these houses are built too close together?

1930s housing.
Questions to ask:
- Describe the differences between these houses and those from Victorian and Edwardian times.
- Do these houses have garages?

London council flats in the 1960s.
Question to ask:
- How many storeys high is this block of flats?

Living Rooms
Pages 6–7

A family at home in Wiltshire in about 1900.
Questions to ask:
- Describe some of the furniture you can see.
- What are the curtains and rugs made from?

A family in their one-room home in London – date unknown.
Questions to ask:
- How can you tell that the family sleep and eat in this room?
- Describe the decoration.

A family at home in the 1940s.
Questions to ask:
- Do you think this room looks modern or old-fashioned?
- Describe the wallpaper.

Cooking in the Kitchen
Pages 8–9

The late Victorian scullery at the birthplace of the composer, Holst.
Questions to ask:
- Do you think this kitchen looks modern or old-fashioned?
- Can you name any of the utensils in this kitchen?

The scullery of a typical Victorian or Edwardian terraced house.
Question to ask:
- Besides the washing and washing-up, what else do you think people did in this scullery?

A kitchen from 1967.
Question to ask:
- Do you think this kitchen looks modern or old-fashioned?

Bedrooms Through the Ages
Pages 10–11

A painting of a nursery by Fritz von Uhde from 1889.
Questions to ask:
- Describe the furniture in this picture.
- How is the room decorated?

A mother of twenty children tucks her children into bed.
Questions to ask:
- Do you think these little girls were comfortable in bed?
- Describe their bed clothes.

French teenagers in their bedroom *circa* 1950s or 1960s.
Questions to ask:
- Describe the decoration.
- Do you have friends around to play in your bedroom? What kind of games do you play?

Bathrooms and Toilets
Pages 12–13

An advertisement for Sadia water heaters.
Question to ask:
- How is the water in your house heated?

No information about this picture.
Questions to ask:
- Would you like to bath like this?
- How is the man hidden from the girls?

A communal outside toilet in Liverpool in 1957.
Question to ask:
- Describe this toilet. Do you think it looks comfortable?

Home Comforts
Pages 14–15

An advertisement for Rippingille's oil stoves from 1894.
Questions to ask:
- How many oil heaters can you see in this picture?
- Can you see any other appliances that use oil in this picture?

An advertisement for Xcel electrical appliances from the 1930s.
Question to ask:
- Do these electrical appliances look modern or old-fashioned?

A woman with a vacuum cleaner in 1954. At that time it would have cost about £29.
Question to ask:
- Do you think the vacuum cleaner looks old-fashioned?

Decoration and Furniture
Pages 16–17

A drawing room in Grosvenor Square in London in 1880.
Questions to ask:
- Describe the kind of furniture in this picture.
- Do you think the room would have been warm?

A drawing room from 1929 from a picture by K. Bentson.
Questions to ask:
- Do you think this room looks modern or old-fashioned?
- What colours can you see?

The cover from *Homemaker* magazine in 1959.
Question to ask:
- What are the people doing in this picture?

A Space Outside
Pages 18–19

Slums in Shoreditch in London in 1922.
Questions to ask:
- Besides the washing what else did these people do in their backyards?
- Do you think it looks clean?

Planting vegetables during the Second World War.
Question to ask:
- What kind of vegetables are growing in this picture?

Girls sitting on their balcony in Camden in London.
Questions to ask:
- Is there a balcony above the one the girls are sitting on?
- Do you think there is enough room for garden furniture on this balcony?

Glossary

advertisement Words and pictures that are used to sell something to people.

backyard The small space, often with a hard surface, outside a house.

balconies A small space on the outside of a building, usually on an upper level.

bungalow A small house with one storey or level.

cast-iron range A stove that uses a fire to heat food.

central heating A system that heats water or air. The heated air or water is then carried around a building through pipes and radiators to heat up the whole place.

cluttered When a room is full of things and there is not much room.

do-it-yourself (DIY) Describes any work that is done on the home, such as decorating or building work, by somebody who lives there.

Edwardian Used to describe anything or anyone from the time of King Edward VII (1901–1910).

electrical appliance A machine that is designed to do a certain job, such as cleaning or cooking.

fitted Describes the specially designed furniture that goes in a kitchen.

high-rise A very tall building with many floors or levels. There are usually flats on each floor.

material The cloth or substance from which something is made. Cotton, silk, wood and plastic are different kinds of material.

microwave An electric oven that cooks by passing microwaves, or electro-magnetic waves, through the food.

modern Describes something that is new or up-to-date.

nursery A room in the home where young children eat, play and sleep. Can also be a place outside the home where children are looked after while their parents are working.

record player An electrical machine used for playing musical records before stereos were invented.

relax/relaxed/relaxing To rest and take things easy.

scullery A small room at the back of a house where dishes and clothes were washed.

Second World War The world war that started in 1939 and ended in 1945.

secure Describes something that is safe and well-protected.

slum An overcrowded, poor and run-down part of a town or city.

stove A piece of equipment used for heating and cooking. In the past coal or wood was burned to create heat. In later times electricity or gas were used.

tank A large container for liquids.

Victorian Used to describe anything or anyone from the time when Queen Victoria ruled Britain (1837–1901).

wallpaper Strips of patterned or coloured paper that are used to decorate a room.

Further Information

Books to Read
Non-fiction
Fifty Years Ago: At Home by Karen Bryant-Mole (Wayland, 1998)
Houses and Homes by Tim Wood (Heinemann, 1995)
Start Up History: Homes by Stewart Ross (Evans, 2002)

Fiction
Anna Then and Anna Now by Josette Blanco and Claude d'Ham (Young Library, 1989)
Stephen Then, Stephen Now by Josette Blanco and Claude d'Ham (Young Library, 1989)

Website for Teachers
http://www.educate.org.uk/teacher _zone/classroom/history/unit2.htm
What were homes like a long time ago? This unit looks at similarities and differences between homes today and homes in the past. Features of buildings, household objects and stories about home life are used to help children to develop the ability to distinguish old from new, and to learn about life in the past.

Museums to Visit
Victoria and Albert Museum
National Museum of Art and Design
Cromwell Road, South Kensington
London SW7 2RL
Tel: 020 7942 2000

The Black Country Living Museum
Tipton Road, Dudley, West Midlands
DY1 4SQ
Tel: 0121 557 9643

Beamish,
County Durham
DH9 0RG
Tel: 01207 231811

The People's Story Museum
Canongate Tolbooth
163 Canongate
Royal Mile
Edinburgh
EH8 8DD
Tel: 0131 529 4057

Index

advertisements 14, 15

backyards 18
balconies 19
bath 12
bathrooms 12, 13
bed 11
bedrooms 10, 11
bungalows 4

caravans 4
carpets 15
cast-iron ranges 8, 12, 14
central heating 14
cleaning 9
computers 10
cooking 7, 8
cottages 4
cupboards 9
curtains 16, 17

decorating 17
decoration 16, 17
dishwashers 14
do-it-yourself (DIY) 17

eating 10
Edwardians 4, 18
electrical appliances 8, 14, 15

electric fire 15
electric heater 12
electricity 17

fire 8, 13
fireplace 7
flats 4, 5
flowers 18, 19
fridges 9
friends 10
furniture 16, 17

games 6, 10
gardens 5, 18, 19
garden furniture 18, 19

houses 4

kitchens 8, 9, 12

lawns 18
lessons 10
living rooms 6
lounge 6

materials 16, 17
meals 6, 10
microwaves 14
music 11

nursery 10

oil heaters 14

paints 16
patios 18
piano 6

radios 6, 7
reading 6, 7
record players 11
relaxing 6, 7, 14

scullery 9, 12
Second World War 19
shower 12
sink 9
sleeping 7, 10
slums 4
stoves 8, 12

television 6, 7, 10
toilets 12, 13, 18
toys 10

vacuum cleaner 15
Victorians 4, 6, 8, 10, 12, 14, 16, 17, 18

wallpapers 16
washing 8, 18
washing-up 9
water supply 12